LOW COS

Mid-week Me

GW00363356

Energy and enthusiasm for cooking frequently flag by the middle of the week. To counter that well-worn refrain, 'What shall we have for dinner tonight?' this book provides a collection of dishes that are as interesting as they are easy to prepare.

When you've spent a busy day, the last thing you want to do is spend hours preparing food. Recipes range from simple fish dishes that can be prepared in less time than it takes to set the table, to slow-cooked stews that can be left to look after themselves while you do something more interesting.

The collection includes simple supper dishes for those occasions when you've had a hearty lunch, main course salads for light summer evenings and more substantial offerings for nights when there's a nip in the air.

Food fatigue – that boredom with the familiar – is overcome by presenting old favourites in new guises: Meatloaf appears with a fancy pastry coat; meatballs, pepped up with cheese, find an affinity with savoury lentils; frankfurters make a satisfying and nourishing family meal when combined with barley; chicken drumsticks, those stalwart supporters of the mid-week menu, gain a new lease of life with a polenta crust.

Fresh fruit makes the perfect finale to a mid-week meal. Simple combinations, such as fanned slices of pineapple with orange segments, or black grapes with melon balls, can be highly successful.

CONTENTS

SUCCULENT SEAFOOD

Fish makes a tasty, satisfying meal. Cheap oily fish such as mackerel and herring are delicious simply sprinkled with fresh herbs, or spread with mustard and grilled or baked in the oven. Many of the fish on the following pages may be interchanged according to what is in season and the best buy. Try mouthwatering combinations such as Trout with Citrus Ginger Sauce, Plaice Fillets with Pear Sauce, or Fish with Green Peppercorn Sauce.

Pan-fried Whiting Fillets

8 x 60g (2oz) whiting fillets

90g (3oz) flour

2 eggs, beaten

125g (4oz) dried breadcrumbs

125g (4oz) butter

herb sprigs for garnish

1 Dredge fillets in the flour, dip in egg, then coat in breadcrumbs.

2 Melt the butter in a large frying pan over moderate heat, add fillets and cook for 3-5 minutes each side or until cooked through. Serve immediately garnished with fresh herbs.

Serves 4

Marinated Fish Fillets

500g (1lb) whiting or other white fish fillets

flour

salt

freshly ground black pepper

oil for deep-frying

white wine vinegar

3 tblspn chopped fresh parsley

1 tblspn chopped fresh marjoram

1 Cut fish fillets into 2.5 x 5cm (1 x 2in) strips. Dust strips with flour seasoned with salt and pepper.

2 Deep fry fish in batches in hot oil for about 2 minutes until golden and cooked through. Drain on paper towels, then place in a dish.

3 Pour over enough white wine vinegar to cover the fish, stir in parsley and marjoram. Cover and refrigerate for 24 hours.

4 Allow fish to return to room temperature before serving.

Serves 4

Pan-fried Whiting Fillets

Herring Parcels

4 large herring fillets, skinned

2 sheets ready-rolled frozen puff pastry, thawed

4 slices tomato

1 egg, beaten

Filling

1 tblspn oil

1 onion, thinly sliced

2 tspn grated lemon rind

1 tblspn chopped fresh parsley

8 black olives, stoned and chopped

1 Preheat oven to 190° C (375°F, Gas 5). Make filling: Heat oil in a frying pan, add onion, stir fry until tender, then drain on paper towels. Combine onion with lemon rind, parsley and olives.

2 Remove any remaining bones from fish fillets, cut each fillet crosswise in half. Cut pastry sheets in half to make 4 rectangles.

3 Place half a fillet on the centre of one rectangle of pastry. Top with one quarter of the filling and a slice of tomato. Top with half a fish fillet.

4 Brush edges of pastry with a little water, bring edges together to form a parcel, pressing together well to seal completely. Repeat with remaining ingredients to make 4 parcels.

5 Place parcels seam side down on a greased baking sheet. Decorate with extra pastry cut into leaf shapes if liked. Cut 2 holes in each parcel to allow steam to escape. Brush with beaten egg, bake in oven for 5 minutes, then reduce oven temperature to 180°C (350°F, Gas 4) and bake a further 15 minutes or until golden brown.

Serves 4

Variations

If preferred, substitute a 410g (13oz) can of drained tuna, pink salmon or mackerel fillets for the herring fillets.

Tasty additions to the filling include sweetcorn, tomato or cucumber relish, chopped fresh tarragon, chives or dill, or tartare sauce. For spicy fish parcels add 1 teaspoon curry powder when frying the onion for the filling. Omit the olives.

Haddock with Tahini Topping

4 haddock fillets

salt

1 onion, thinly sliced

60ml (2fl oz) olive oil

45g (1½oz) pinenuts

3 tblspn chopped fresh mint

freshly ground black pepper

Tahini Topping

60g (2oz) tahini

125ml (4fl oz) water

juice of 1 lemon

1 clove garlic, finely chopped

1 Preheat oven to 180°C (350°F, Gas 4). Dry fish with paper towels. Season lightly with salt, then place in an ovenproof baking dish.

2 Sauté onion in 1 tablespoon of the oil for about 5 minutes until golden. Add pinenuts and sauté for 1 minute. Add the mint and pepper to taste, then spoon over fish.

3 Sprinkle remaining oil over fish and bake in oven for 15-20 minutes or until fish flakes easily.

4 Meanwhile, combine tahini, water, lemon juice and garlic in a small bowl. About 5 minutes before the end of cooking time, spoon the mixture over fish and complete cooking. Serve hot.

Serves 4

Herring Parcels

John Dory and Spinach Rolls

John Dory and Spinach Rolls

60ml (2fl oz) lemon juice

1/4 tspn crushed black peppercorns

2 cloves garlic, crushed

8 John Dory fillets

16 spinach leaves, stems removed

60g (2oz) butter, melted

1 tblspn snipped fresh chives for garnish

1 Preheat oven to 180°C (350°F, Gas 4). Combine lemon juice, black pepper and garlic and brush over fish. Lay 2 spinach leaves (cut to size) on each fillet. Roll up and secure with a cocktail stick.

2 Place fish in a baking dish, brush with butter and bake for 20 minutes or until cooked through. Garnish with chives and serve.

Serves 4

Fish with Green Peppercorn Sauce

125ml (4fl oz) fish stock

125ml (4fl oz) dry white wine

250ml (8fl oz) double cream

4 x 185g (6oz) firm white fish fillets

salt

90g (3oz) butter, cubed

1 tblspn bottled green peppercorns, drained and rinsed

1 Preheat oven to 200°C (400°F, Gas 6). Combine stock and wine in a small saucepan. Reduce by half over high heat. Add cream and reduce to about 155ml (5fl oz). Set aside and keep warm.

2 Butter 4 pieces of foil large enough to hold fillets. Place fillets on foil, season with salt, add remaining butter cubes, and seal foil packets securely.

3 Place foil packets on a baking sheet and cook for 12 minutes until fish flakes easily.

4 When ready to serve, add green peppercorns to sauce and warm through. Remove fish from foil pour over sauce and serve.

Serves 4

Plaice Fillets with Pear Sauce

15g (1/2oz) butter

4 small plaice fillets

4 spring onions, chopped

2 pears, peeled, cored and sliced

60ml (2fl oz) dry white wine

60ml (2fl oz) low fat natural yogurt

salt

freshly ground black pepper

1 Melt butter in a frying pan, add fillets and fry gently for 8 minutes, turning once. Remove from pan and keep warm.

2 Add spring onions to pan, sauté for 3 minutes, add pear slices and cook until just tender.

3 Stir wine and yogurt into pan and heat through gently. Season to taste. Return fillets to pan and reheat gently.

Serves 4

Cod Steaks with Mustard Butter

90g (3oz) butter, at room temperature

1 tblspn wholegrain mustard

1/2 small onion, finely chopped

salt

freshly ground black pepper

4 x 185g (6oz) cod or swordfish steaks

2 tblspn olive oil

1 Combine butter, mustard and onion in a bowl, beat to mix and season with salt and pepper.

2 Brush fish with 1 tablespoon of oil. Use remaining oil to brush grill tray.

3 Cook fish under a preheated grill for 6 minutes or until just cooked, turning once.

4 Place a quarter of the butter mixture on each fish steak and return briefly to grill until butter is bubbling.

Serves 4

Trout with Citrus Ginger Sauce

30g (1oz) butter
2 small trout, cleaned and trimmed
1 tblspn fresh root ginger, peeled and finely sliced
60ml (2fl oz) orange juice
15g (1/2oz) brown sugar
strips of lime rind for garnish

1 Melt butter in a frying pan. Add trout and cook for 3 minutes each side or until cooked through. Remove trout and keep warm.

2 Add remaining ingredients to pan and cook sauce for 10 minutes, or until slightly thickened. Pour sauce over trout and garnish with strips of lime rind.

Serves 2

Fish Pie

500g (1lb) cooked white fish
375g (12oz) potatoes, cooked and mashed
185g (6oz) carrots, cooked and mashed
1 tblspn chopped fresh parsley
30g (1oz) fresh breadcrumbs
30g (1oz) butter, melted

1 Preheat oven to 180°C (350°F, Gas 4). Flake fish.

2 Combine mashed potato and carrots, spread half the mixture over the base of a greased ovenproof dish.

3 Arrange fish on top, sprinkle with parsley. Cover with remaining potato mixture.

4 Combine breadcrumbs and butter and sprinkle over the potato mixture. Bake for 15 minutes until bubbling hot and golden.

Serves 4

Fish with Sweetcorn

1 x 350g (11oz) can sweetcorn, drained
1 tspn arrowroot or cornflour
125ml (4fl oz) vegetable or tomato juice
4 small cod steaks
1 tblspn oil
2 tblspn chopped fresh parsley for garnish

1 Place sweetcorn in a blender or food processor with arrowroot or cornflour. Add vegetable or tomato juice and blend until smooth.

2 Brush cod with oil and place in a shallow flameproof dish. Cook cod in dish under a hot grill for 2 minutes, turn over and grill for a further 1 minute. Pour over corn mixture.

3 Grill for a further 10 minutes or until cod is cooked through and sweetcorn mixture thickens slightly and browns. Sprinkle with parsley.

Serves 4

Fish Pie

ECONOMICAL MEAT DISHES

Even the toughest, most economical cuts of meat can be rendered moist and tender with long, slow cooking, and more expensive choice cuts can be 'stretched' with other ingredients. On the following pages you will find a mouthwatering array of succulent meat dishes – from soups to stews – including Beef, Mushroom and Mustard Pie, Pork Vindaloo and Super Simple Meatloaf.

Hearty Beef and Brussels Sprout Soup

2 tblspn oil

500g (1lb) stewing steak, cut into 2.5cm (1in) cubes

1 onion, chopped

3 cloves garlic, crushed

60ml (2fl oz) sherry

1.5 litres (2¹/₂pt) chicken or beef stock

315g (10oz) new potatoes, sliced

125g (4oz) carrots, sliced

1 tspn dried rosemary

125g (4oz) Brussels sprouts, halved

¹/₂ tspn crushed black peppercorns

1 Heat oil in a large, deep saucepan over high heat. Add the beef and stir until browned on all sides. Stir in the onion and garlic and cook for a further 1 minute, then add the sherry.

2 Pour the stock into the pan, bring to the boil, then simmer, partially covered, for 1 hour.

3 Add the potatoes, carrots and rosemary and simmer for a further 10 minutes. Stir in the Brussels sprouts and black pepper. Cook for 5 minutes or until sprouts are tender.

Serves 4

Kitchen Tip

The cheapest meats are usually those cuts which have long, coarse muscle fibres and more gristle than leaner, more expensive cuts. They can be rendered tender by slow, moist methods of cooking. Pounding the meat with a meat mallet also helps to tenderise it, as does marinating it in a citrus marinade. Tougher cuts may also be minced to break up the muscle fibres, enabling them to be cooked by quicker methods.

Hearty Beef and Brussels Sprout Soup

Shepherd's Pie

Shepherd's Pie

2 tblspn olive oil

1 onion, chopped

2 cloves garlic, crushed

125g (4oz) rindless bacon, chopped

750g (1¹/₂lb) minced lamb or beef

3 tblspn tomato purée

1 tblspn dried mixed herbs

2 tblspn Worcestershire sauce

2 tspn brown sugar

185ml (6fl oz) red wine

4 large potatoes, peeled and chopped

30g (1oz) butter

¹/₄ tspn grated nutmeg

60ml (2fl oz) milk

pinch paprika

1 Preheat oven to 180°C (350°F, Gas 4). Heat oil in a large, nonstick frying pan over moderate heat, add the onion, garlic and bacon and cook for 2 minutes. Stir in the mince and brown well. Drain excess oil. Add tomato purée, herbs, Worcestershire sauce and sugar. Stir in wine, bring to the boil, then simmer for 30 minutes.

2 Spoon mixture into a blender or food processor and blend for 2-3 seconds, to break up any large lumps, but do not purée. Spread mixture in an ovenproof dish.

3 Cook potatoes in a saucepan of boiling water until tender, drain. Mash potatoes with half the butter, nutmeg and milk. Top mince with the potato mixture. Sprinkle with paprika and dot with remaining butter. Bake for 25 minutes until heated and golden.

Serves 6

Variation
Shepherd's Pie is an ideal way of using leftover cooked meat from a joint, or leftover vegetables. Try these delicious variations on the basic recipe:
Flavour the minced lamb with 1 tblspn chopped fresh sage, or 1 tspn dried sage, or 2 tspn curry powder. Top with a layer of steamed sliced courgettes, then mashed potato. Add 2 tblspn creamed horseradish sauce to the mixture if using beef. Top with combined mashed potatoes and parsnips and sprinkle with grated cheese of your choice.
Use minced pork and add 1 peeled and chopped apple, or 1 tblspn redcurrant jelly. Top with a layers of mashed swede or turnip, and potato.

Chilli Minced Beef with Carrots

Chilli Minced Beef with Carrots

1 tblspn vegetable oil

500g (1lb) minced beef

1 x 440g (14oz) can chopped tomatoes

1 tspn ground cinnamon

1/2 tspn crushed black peppercorns

1 tspn chilli paste

125ml (4fl oz) tomato purée

2 tspn brown sugar

60ml (2fl oz) dry sherry

750g (1¹/2lb) carrots, peeled and chopped

15g (¹/2oz) butter

¹/4 tspn grated nutmeg

2 tblspn single cream

chives for garnish

1 Heat the oil in a large, nonstick frying pan over moderate heat. Add beef and brown, breaking up any lumps with a wooden spoon. Stir in the tomatoes, cinnamon, black pepper, chilli paste, tomato purée, sugar and sherry, bring to the boil, then simmer for 35 minutes, stirring occasionally.

2 Boil or steam carrots until tender, then mash with the butter, nutmeg and cream until smooth. Serve the mince on a bed of mashed carrots, garnished with chives.

Serves 4

Lentils with Meatballs

625g (1¹/4lb) minced lamb

30g (1oz) fresh breadcrumbs

30g (1oz) grated Parmesan cheese

2 tblspn chopped fresh parsley

2 tspn olive oil

1 leek, sliced

2 carrots, chopped

2 sticks celery, sliced

4 cloves garlic, crushed

1 bay leaf

410g (13oz) Continental lentils

salt

1 litre (1³/4pt) chicken stock

1 Combine lamb, breadcrumbs, Parmesan and parsley in a bowl. Form the mixture into 12 equal balls, then refrigerate for 30 minutes until firm.

2 Heat oil in a large, heavy-based frying pan, add meatballs and brown on all sides over high heat for about 4 minutes. Remove from pan with a slotted spoon and set aside. Add leek, carrots, celery, garlic and bay leaf to the pan, sauté over a gentle heat for about 10 minutes until soft.

3 Add lentils to pan with salt to taste and stock. Stir, then bring to the boil. Add meatballs, partially cover the pan and simmer for about 45 minutes until the meatballs and lentils are tender. Add a little hot water if mixture becomes too dry during cooking. Serve hot.

Serves 6

Creamy Sausage and Bean-filled Red Peppers

4 medium red peppers
2 tspn vegetable oil
1 onion, finely chopped
3 cloves garlic, crushed
4 chipolata sausages, poached, drained and roughly chopped
2 tspn dried coriander
1 x 220g (7oz) can chopped tomatoes
2 tspn tomato purée
2 tspn ground cumin
1 x 220g (7oz) can red kidney beans, drained
250ml (8fl oz) double cream
90g (3oz) cooked rice
chopped fresh parsley for garnish

1 Preheat oven to 180°C (350°F, Gas 4). Slice red peppers horizontally in half, cut out seeds and inner membranes and take a thin slice off bottoms so they sit upright. Heat the oil in a large, nonstick frying pan over moderate heat, add the onion and garlic and cook for 3 minutes.

2 Add sausages, coriander, tomatoes, tomato purée, cumin, beans and cream to the pan. Cook for 20 minutes over high heat, stirring occasionally or until cream begins to thicken.

3 Stir in the rice and spoon mixture into prepared red pepper shells, stand in a baking dish and bake in oven for 25 minutes until peppers are tender. Serve garnished with parsley.

Serves 4

Creamy Sausage and Bean-filled Red Peppers

Creamy Kidneys in Puff Pastry Cases

Creamy Kidneys in Puff Pastry Cases

10 lambs' kidneys

2 tblspn olive oil

1 onion, chopped

250ml (8fl oz) chicken stock

60ml (2fl oz) port or red wine

1 tblspn tomato purée

2 tspn cornflour mixed with 2 tblspn cold water

1 tblspn redcurrant jelly

2 tblspn soured cream

2 sheets ready-rolled frozen puff pastry, thawed

strips of red pepper and watercress sprigs for garnish

1 Soak kidneys in boiling water for 2 minutes, then drain. Remove skins and any gristle, and cut into bite-sized pieces. Heat oil in a nonstick frying pan over moderate heat then stir in kidneys and onion and cook for 5 minutes. Transfer to plate and keep warm.

2 Add stock and port or red wine to the frying pan and boil until reduced by half. Stir in tomato purée, cornflour mixture and redcurrant jelly and cook for a further 3 minutes. Stir in soured cream with kidney and onion mixture and remove from heat.

3 Cut pastry into rounds large enough to line the bottom and sides of 4 individual loose-bottomed flan tins. Prick the bases of the flans with a fork and bake pastry in oven for 10-12 minutes or until cooked. When cooked, push down any risen pastry and cool slightly before removing pastry from the tins. Gently reheat kidney cream filling, fill pastry cases and serve immediately, garnished with red pepper strips and watercress.

Serves 4

Lambs' Kidneys Toscana

500g (1lb) small lambs' kidneys

2 tblspn red wine vinegar

4 tblspn olive oil

3 tblspn finely chopped fresh parsley

2 cloves garlic, finely chopped

6 canned anchovy fillets, drained and pounded to a paste

2 tblspn lemon juice

salt

freshly ground black pepper

1 Remove fat and gristle from the kidneys. Cut them in half and rinse very well under running water. Place in a shallow bowl and pour over vinegar and set aside for 20 minutes. Drain and wash kidneys again, then cut into slices.

2 Heat oil in a large, heavy-based frying pan and cook kidneys for 5 minutes over high heat, stirring constantly. When nearly cooked, add parsley, garlic

12

and anchovies to the pan and stir for a further 2-3 minutes. Sprinkle with lemon juice and season with salt and pepper. Serve.

Serves 4

Spinach Salad with Sautéed Chicken Livers

6 slices white bread, crusts removed
60g (2oz) butter
375g (12oz) chicken livers, trimmed
3 tblspn brandy
1 tblspn dried mixed herbs
16 young spinach leaves, rinsed and dried
60ml (2fl oz) dry white wine
1 tblspn olive oil
1/2 red pepper, finely chopped

1 Using a small metal cutter, cut crescents from the bread. Melt half the butter in a medium frying pan over moderate heat until bubbling. Add bread shapes to the frying pan and cook over gentle heat until the bread is lightly golden. Remove from frying pan.

2 Melt the remaining butter in the frying pan and add chicken livers. Cook for 2 minutes, stirring constantly. Add the brandy and herbs and cook for a further 3 minutes.

3 Arrange spinach leaves on a serving plate. Remove chicken livers from frying pan with a slotted spoon, slice and arrange on the spinach leaves.

4 Add the wine to the pan and cook for 2 minutes. Strain the wine mixture, then add the oil and mix well. Pour dressing over salad and top with the croûtons and red pepper. Serve with French bread for a light supper.

Serves 4

Variations
Add 1 crushed clove of garlic, the grated rind of 1/2 lemon or 1 lime, a dash of Worcestershire sauce or 1 teaspoon of curry powder to the oil when frying the croûtons.
Other decorative shapes may be cut from the bread using aspic cutters or fancy biscuit cutters.

Spinach Salad with Sautéed Chicken Livers

Beef, Mushroom and Mustard Pie

750g (1¹/2lb) rump steak, any visible fat removed, cut into 2.5cm (1in) cubes

2 tblspn flour

2-4 tblspn olive oil

30g (1oz) butter

1 large Spanish onion, coarsely chopped

125g (4oz) rindless bacon, coarsely chopped

185g (6oz) button mushrooms, thickly sliced

250ml (8fl oz) beef stock

3 tblspn Dijon mustard

1 tspn dry English mustard

2 tblspn chopped fresh parsley

1 tblspn chopped fresh thyme

freshly ground black pepper

500g (1lb) shortcrust pastry, thawed if frozen

1 egg yolk mixed with 1 tblspn milk

1 Preheat oven to 220°C (425°F, Gas 7). Dredge beef cubes with flour, shaking off any excess. Heat 2 tablespoons of the oil in a heavy-based frying pan. When very hot, brown meat in batches, until browned on all sides. Use remaining oil if necessary. Set meat aside in a 1.5 litre (2¹/2pt) ovenproof pie dish.

2 Add half the butter to the pan. When melted, sauté onion for about 5 minutes until golden. Remove from pan and add to meat.

3 Add bacon to pan, fry until just crisp, drain on paper towels, add to meat. Melt remaining butter in pan, add mushrooms and toss over a high heat until barely cooked. Add to meat.

4 Pour stock and mustards into the frying pan, bring the boil and add to meat, onion, bacon and mushrooms. Mix well, then add parsley, thyme and black pepper.

5 Roll out the pastry to fit the top of the pie dish, press all along the edge with the prongs of a fork

to seal the pastry. Brush the top of the pie with the egg yolk glaze. Make a small vent in the middle of the pie with a sharp knife and bake in oven for 20 minutes. Reduce oven temperature to 180°C (350°F, Gas 4) and cook for a further 20 minutes until pastry is golden. Serve hot.

Serves 6

Steak and Kidney Pie

750g (1¹/2lb) lean braising steak, trimmed and cut into 2cm (³/4in) cubes

6 lambs' kidneys, cored and roughly chopped

45g (1¹/2oz) flour

1 tblspn vegetable oil

2 cloves garlic, crushed

2 onions, chopped

¹/2 tspn powdered mustard

2 tblspn chopped fresh parsley

2 tblspn Worcestershire sauce

375ml (12fl oz) beef stock

2 tspn tomato purée

500g (1lb) puff pastry, thawed if frozen

2 tblspn milk

1 Coat the steak and kidneys in flour, shake off any excess. Heat oil in a large, nonstick frying pan over high heat. Add steak and kidneys, brown well on all sides. Stir in garlic and onions and cook for a further 3 minutes. Stir in mustard, parsley, Worcestershire sauce, stock and tomato purée, mix well, then cover and simmer for 2¹/2 hours, stirring occasionally. Cool mixture to room temperature. Remove excess fat from surface.

2 Preheat oven to 200°C (400°F, Gas 6). Roll out pastry to fit the top of an ovenproof pie dish. Fill dish with steak and kidney mixture, place pastry on top, trim edges and decorate with extra pastry, if desired.

3 Brush top of pie with milk and bake in oven for 20-25 minutes or until pastry is golden and meat is heated through. Serve immediately.

Serves 6

Steak and Kidney Pie

Peppered Meatloaf Wrapped in Puff Pastry

Peppered Meatloaf Wrapped in Puff Pastry

90g (3oz) butter

2 cloves garlic, crushed

1 large onion, finely chopped

2 tspn dried oregano

60ml (2fl oz) port or red wine

1 tblspn red wine vinegar

1 tspn brown sugar

60g (2oz) dried breadcrumbs

1/2 tspn crushed black peppercorns

875g (1¾lb) minced beef

3 tblspn chopped fresh parsley

1 tblspn bottled green peppercorns, drained

60g (2oz) Cheddar cheese, grated

2 tblspn tomato purée

2 eggs, beaten

500g (1lb) puff pastry, thawed if frozen

1 Preheat oven to 180°C (350°F, Gas 4). Melt 30g (1oz) of the butter in a large frying pan over moderate heat. Stir in garlic, onion and oregano and cook for 3 minutes. Stir in port or red wine, vinegar and sugar and cook for a further 2 minutes. Stir in breadcrumbs and black pepper, then remove from heat. Mix in the beef, parsley, peppercorns, Cheddar, tomato purée and eggs and combine thoroughly.

2 Roll out pastry to a 45cm (18in) square, then cut a 6cm (2½in) square out from each corner. Place meat mixture in a log shape on the centre of pastry, wrap up like a parcel and place seam-side down on a greased baking sheet. Decorate the top with pastry trimmings if liked.

3 Melt remaining butter and brush over the pastry. Bake meatloaf in oven for 1¼ hours, covering with foil during cooking if necessary. Cool loaf on a wire rack for 10 minutes before slicing.

Serves 6

Beef and Tomato Curry

3 tblspn oil

750g (1½lb) braising steak, trimmed and cut into 2cm x 4cm (¾in x 1½in) strips

3 cloves garlic, crushed

3 onions, finely chopped

1 tblspn medium curry powder

1 tblspn cumin seeds

2 tspn ground coriander

2 tblspn tomato purée

1 tblspn sweet fruit chutney

1 x 440g (14oz) can chopped tomatoes

250ml (8fl oz) water

1 Heat the oil in a large frying pan over high heat. Add the beef, garlic and onions and cook for 3 minutes, stirring constantly.

2 Add the curry powder, cumin seeds, coriander, tomato purée, chutney, tomatoes and water. Cover and simmer for 1 hour or until beef is tender, stirring occasionally.

Serves 6

Pork Vindaloo

750g (1½lb) pork, trimmed and cut into small cubes

2 onions, chopped

3 cloves garlic, crushed

1 x 440g (14oz) can chopped tomatoes

2 tspn ground cumin

2 tspn mustard seeds

2 tspn ground cinnamon

1 tspn ground turmeric

½ tspn crushed black peppercorns

1 tspn chilli paste

60ml (2fl oz) white wine vinegar

2 tspn brown sugar

60ml (2fl oz) plain yogurt

2 tblspn freshly squeezed lime juice

375ml-500ml (12fl oz-16fl oz) chicken stock

2 tblspn chopped fresh coriander, plus coriander sprig for garnish

1 Combine pork, onions, garlic, tomatoes, cumin, mustard seeds, cinnamon, turmeric, black pepper, chilli paste, vinegar, sugar, yogurt and lime juice in a large non-metallic bowl and mix well. Cover and marinate for 3 hours or overnight in the refrigerator if possible.

2 Transfer mixture to a large saucepan. Add 375ml (12fl oz) stock. Simmer over moderate heat for 1¼ hours, stirring occasionally, adding more stock or water if necessary. Stir in chopped coriander, and serve with rice. Garnish with coriander sprig.

Serves 6

Beef and Tomato Curry, Pork Vindaloo

Tomato Steak Casserole

2 tblspn olive oil

1 onion, chopped

2 cloves garlic, crushed

500g (1lb) small new potatoes, halved

1kg (2lb) chuck steak, fat removed and cut into 4cm (1¹/₂in) cubes

500ml (16fl oz) red wine

2 tblspn tomato purée

1 x 440g (14oz) can chopped tomatoes

750ml (1¹/₄pt) chicken stock

4 sticks celery, finely chopped

1 Heat the oil in a large, deep frying pan over moderate heat. Add the onion, garlic and potatoes and cook for 7 minutes, stirring constantly.

2 Add the steak pieces to the pan and brown on all sides. Stir in the wine, tomato purée, tomatoes and stock and bring mixture to the boil, then cover and simmer for 1¹/₄ hours, stirring occasionally. Stir in the celery and serve.

Serves 8

Kitchen Tip
If small new potatoes are not in season, use potatoes cut into large chunks, or into 2.5cm (1in) thick slices.

Super Simple Meatloaf

30g (1oz) butter

1 onion, finely chopped

1kg (2lb) minced pork

2 eggs, lightly beaten

1 tblspn Dijon mustard

60g (2oz) fresh breadcrumbs

salt

freshly ground black pepper

grated nutmeg

Tomato Steak Casserole

1 Preheat oven to 160°C (325°F, Gas 3). Melt butter in a small frying pan, add onion and sauté for about 5 minutes until golden.

2 Place mince in a mixing bowl, add onion, eggs, mustard and breadcrumbs. Mix well. Season to taste with salt, pepper and nutmeg.

3 Place mixture in a lightly greased 1kg (2lb) loaf pan, pressing down well. Bake in oven for about 1 hour until cooked through.

4 Turn meatloaf out onto a serving plate, and serve warm or cold.

Serves 6

Pork Rissoles with Red Pepper Sauce

500g (1lb) minced pork
salt
freshly ground black pepper
grated nutmeg
1 egg, beaten
45g (1½oz) flour for dredging, plus 1 tblspn
60g (2oz) butter
1 small onion, finely chopped
1 red pepper, cut into 5mm (¼in) cubes
1 tblspn mild paprika
185ml (6fl oz) chicken stock
Worcestershire sauce
100ml (3½fl oz) single cream

1 Put mince in a mixing bowl, season with salt, pepper and nutmeg. Add enough egg to bind. Shape mixture into 4 patties, dredge with flour and shake off any excess.

2 Melt butter in a large saucepan. When foam starts to subside add patties, brown well on both sides. Reduce heat and cook patties for about 30 minutes, turning once. Remove from pan and keep warm.

3 Add onion and red pepper to pan, sauté for about 5 minutes until onion is golden. Stir in remaining tablespoon of flour and paprika, then add stock all at once. Stir over moderate heat until sauce thickens.

4 Season sauce to taste with Worcestershire sauce and salt and pepper. Stir in cream, heat through gently without boiling and serve sauce with rissoles.

Serves 4

Glazed Spareribs

250ml (8fl oz) bottled teriyaki marinade
15g (½oz) brown sugar
2kg (4lb) rack pork spareribs
125g (4oz) orange marmalade

1 Preheat oven to 160°C (325°F, Gas 3). Mix marinade with sugar. Pour over spareribs and allow to marinate 3-4 hours or overnight, turning occasionally.

2 Remove meat from marinade and reserve marinade. Pat meat dry and place on a wire rack in a roasting tin. Cover and cook 1 hour or until cooked, turning once. Increase oven temperature to 190°C (375°F, Gas 5).

3 Combine reserved marinade and marmalade and brush over the meat. Cook in oven for a further 10 minutes or until well browned. Cut racks into serving portions and serve immediately.

Serves 4

Leek and Ham Pie

Pork Strips with Mustard Cream Sauce

30g (1oz) butter

1 tblspn oil

750g (1¹/2lb) pork fillet, trimmed and cut into strips

250ml (8fl oz) dry white wine

2 tblspn Dijon mustard

375ml (12fl oz) double cream

1 Melt butter and oil in a large frying pan over moderate heat. Add pork and cook for 10 minutes, turning frequently.

2 Stir in wine and mustard. Add cream and increase heat, cook for 10 minutes or until mixture thickens.

Serves 4

Thyme Pork Steaks with Apples

4 boneless pork shoulder steaks, 2cm (³/4in) thick

30g (1oz) flour

60g (2oz) butter

2 tblspn finely chopped fresh thyme

2 apples, unpeeled, cut into thin slices

1 Lightly dredge the pork steaks with the flour. Melt the butter in a large frying pan over moderate heat. Cook pork for 2 minutes each side.

2 Sprinkle the thyme over each steak and cook for 3-5 minutes more on each side or until cooked through. Remove pork and keep warm.

3 Using the same frying pan, sauté apples for 2 minutes or until just tender, but not mushy. Arrange pork steaks and apples on a serving plate and serve.

Serves 4

Leek and Ham Pie

500g (1lb) puff pastry, thawed if frozen

2 tblspn vegetable oil

375g (12oz) cooked ham, chopped

2 cloves garlic, crushed

375g (12oz) leeks, sliced

1 red pepper, chopped

155g (5oz) cream cheese

2 eggs

60ml (2fl oz) milk

¹/4 tspn grated nutmeg

50g (13/4oz) Danish Blue cheese

milk to glaze

1 Preheat oven to 190°C (375°F, Gas 5). Roll out enough pastry to line the base and sides of a 22cm (8³/4in) round flan dish. Reserve enough pastry for the top.

2 Place a sheet of baking paper on top of pastry, top with dried beans or baking beans and bake blind for 10 minutes. Remove baking paper and beans, reduce oven temperature to 180°C (350°F, Gas 4) and cook pastry for a further 10 minutes.

3 Heat oil in a large, frying pan over moderate heat. Add the ham, garlic, leeks and red pepper and cook for 2 minutes. Place cream cheese, eggs, milk, nutmeg and blue cheese in a blender or food processor and blend until smooth. Spoon ham mixture into pastry base then pour over the egg mixture.

4 Roll out pastry to fit top of pie and place over filling. Seal edges with a little milk. Prick top of pie with a fork, brush with milk and bake for 45 minutes until golden. Cool in flan dish for 15 minutes.

Serves 4

Pork Strips with Mustard Cream Sauce, Thyme Pork Steaks with Apples

Moussaka

1kg (2lb) aubergines
salt
125ml (4fl oz) olive oil
1 onion, thinly sliced
750g (1¹/₂lb) minced lamb
1 x 440g (14oz) can chopped tomatoes, drained
2 small cloves garlic, crushed
3 tblspn chopped fresh parsley
salt
freshly ground black pepper
60g (2oz) Cheddar cheese, grated

Sauce

30g (1oz) butter
30g (1oz) flour
600ml (1pt) hot milk
grated nutmeg
2 eggs
30g (1oz) grated Parmesan cheese

1 Preheat oven to 180°C (350°F, Gas 4). Cut aubergines into 1cm (¹/₂in) slices. Place in a colander, sprinkle liberally with salt to help draw out the bitter juices. Leave to drain for 30 minutes.

2 Heat 2 tablespoons of the oil in a flameproof casserole, add the onion and sauté for about 5 minutes until golden. Add the lamb and sauté until light brown. Add tomatoes, garlic and parsley and season with salt and pepper. Reduce heat to a simmer and cook for 15 minutes until the mixture has thickened slightly.

3 Rinse the aubergines under cold running water, dry thoroughly with paper towels. Heat remaining oil in a frying pan and sauté aubergine slices in batches until golden brown on both sides, adding more oil to the frying pan if necessary. Remove slices with a slotted spoon, drain on paper towels.

4 Make a layer of aubergine slices in a baking dish. Follow with a layer of meat, and then grated Cheddar. Repeat layering ending with a layer of aubergines.

5 To make the sauce, melt the butter in a saucepan, add flour and cook 2 minutes, stirring constantly. Off the heat, whisk in the milk all at once, then return to the heat and cook until sauce boils and thickens, stirring constantly. Season with salt, pepper and nutmeg and simmer sauce for a further 5 minutes. Beat the eggs in a bowl, whisk in 4 tblspn of the sauce, then return this to the saucepan and stir in well.

6 Spoon sauce over the top layer of aubergine slices, sprinkle with Parmesan. Bake in oven for about 45 minutes until bubbling and golden brown. Serve hot.

Serves 6

Barley and Frankfurter Casserole

45g (1¹/₂oz) butter
1 onion, chopped
250g (8oz) mushrooms, sliced
60g (2oz) rindless bacon, chopped
185g (6oz) barley, soaked in water for 2 hours and then drained
750ml (1¹/₄pt) chicken stock
185ml (6fl oz) dry white wine
1 tspn ground cumin
¹/₂ tspn ground coriander
125ml (4fl oz) single cream
500g (1lb) thin frankfurters, cut into 2cm (³/₄in) lengths
coriander or parsley sprig for garnish

1 Melt the butter in a large frying pan over moderate heat. Add the onion, mushrooms and bacon and cook for 3 minutes, stirring constantly.

2 Add the barley, stock, wine, cumin and coriander and simmer mixture for about 30 minutes until stock has been absorbed.

3 Stir in the cream and frankfurters and cook for a further 10 minutes. Serve garnished with coriander or parsley.

Serves 4

Barley and Frankfurter Casserole

Cassoulet

750g (1½lb) dried haricot beans

250g (8oz) piece of smoked bacon

500g (1lb) boned shoulder of pork

2 tblspn olive oil

2 onions, thinly sliced

4 cloves garlic, finely chopped

1 small shoulder of lamb, boned

500g (1lb) coarse pork and garlic sausage

4 tblspn tomato purée

1.8 litres (3pt) cold water, plus water for soaking

salt

freshly ground black pepper

1 bouquet garni

185g (6oz) fresh breadcrumbs

1 Place beans in a large saucepan. Cover with cold water, bring to the boil, then simmer for 5 minutes. Remove from heat, cover and soak for 45 minutes. Meanwhile, remove rind from bacon and shoulder of pork and cut rind into 5mm (¼in) cubes.

2 Preheat oven to 150°C (300°F, Gas 2). Heat oil in a frying pan, add onions and garlic and sauté until golden. Add rind cubes and sauté for 5 minutes.

3 Raise heat, add bacon and pork, lamb and sausage in turn to brown on all sides. Remove each from pan, and set aside.

4 Stir tomato purée into pan with a little of the water, then bring to the boil, scraping up any browned bits.

5 Drain beans, rinse under cold running water, drain again and return to a clean pan with the remaining cold water. Bring to the boil, then pour beans and water into a large ovenproof casserole. Add liquid contents of the frying pan and season.

6 Add bacon, pork, lamb and sausage; spoon beans over, add bouquet garni, bring to a simmer over a moderate heat.

7 Sprinkle with 125g (4oz) of the breadcrumbs, place uncovered casserole in oven and cook for 2½-3 hours until beans and meat are cooked. When a crust forms, press down with a large spoon and add more breadcrumbs and return to oven. Before serving, cut up the large pieces of meat and sausage.

Serves 12

Lamb Patties with Mint Chutney

500g (1lb) minced lamb

1 onion, finely chopped

15g (½oz) fresh breadcrumbs

1 tblspn tomato purée

Mint Chutney

45g (1½oz) butter

1 onion, chopped

salt

freshly ground black pepper

15g (½oz) brown sugar

3 tblspn white wine vinegar

½ tspn finely chopped fresh mint

1 Combine lamb with onion, breadcrumbs and tomato purée in a bowl, mix well. Shape mixture into 2cm (¾in) thick patties and grill under moderate heat for 5 minutes each side or until cooked through.

2 To make the chutney, melt butter in a medium saucepan over moderate heat, add onion, salt and pepper and cook for 1 minute. Stir in sugar, vinegar and mint. Simmer mixture for 3 minutes, stirring constantly. Add 60ml (2fl oz) water and simmer until mixture has thickened slightly. Serve patties with the chutney.

Serves 4

Lamb and Potato Casserole

1 tblspn vegetable oil

30g (1oz) butter

4 thick lamb chops, all visible fat removed

2 large leeks, thickly sliced

6 potatoes, peeled and thinly sliced

salt

freshly ground black pepper

2 tblspn finely chopped fresh parsley

2 tblspn finely chopped fresh mint

1 clove garlic, halved

1 tblspn redcurrant jelly

500ml (16fl oz) chicken stock

1 Preheat oven to 180°C (350°F, Gas 4). Heat the oil and half the butter in a heavy-based frying pan. Add lamb chops and brown on both sides. Remove chops and discard all but 1 tablespoon fat.

2 Sauté leeks in remaining fat until transparent. Set aside. Add potatoes, salt, pepper, parsley and mint. Mix together gently.

3 Butter a shallow baking dish, rub with cut sides of garlic. Spoon half the potato and herbs into the dish, then arrange chops on top. Place a teaspoon of redcurrant jelly on each chop. Cover with remaining potato mixture. Pour over enough stock to cover potatoes. Dot with remaining butter. Bake, uncovered, for 50 minutes or until most of the liquid has been absorbed and potatoes are cooked and golden.

Serves 4

Lamb with Creamy Mustard Sauce

2 tblspn vegetable oil

1.5kg (3lb) boned leg of lamb, cut into thin strips

2 tspn ground cumin

2 large onions, cut into wedges

3 tblspn wholegrain mustard

2 cloves garlic, crushed

1 tspn chilli paste

250ml (8fl oz) dry white wine

600ml (1pt) chicken stock

2 tblspn cornflour mixed with 75ml (2½fl oz) cold water

60ml (2fl oz) soured cream

2 tblspn chopped fresh parsley

1 Heat the oil in a large, nonstick frying pan over high heat. Add the lamb and brown on all sides.

2 Reduce heat to moderate, stir in cumin, onions, mustard, garlic and chilli paste and cook for 4 minutes. Add wine and simmer for 5 minutes, scraping up any browned bits.

3 Transfer mixture to a large saucepan, stir in stock and cornflour mixture, cover and simmer for 1¹/₂ hours. Remove from heat, stir in soured cream and parsley.

Serves 8

Lamb Hot Pot

500g (1lb) potatoes, peeled and cut into 5mm (¹/₄in) thick slices

500g (1lb) lamb fillets, cut into 1cm (¹/₂in) thick slices

8 lambs' kidneys, cut crosswise in half, soaked in cold water for 30 minutes and then drained

1 tblspn cornflour mixed with 60ml (2fl oz) cold water

250ml (8fl oz) chicken stock

4 cloves garlic, crushed

2 tblspn chopped fresh parsley

125ml (4fl oz) dry white wine

2 tspn dried rosemary

1 tspn crushed black peppercorns

30g (1oz) butter, melted

1 Preheat oven to 180°C (350°F, Gas 4). Place a layer of potato slices, overlapping slightly, on the bottom of an ovenproof casserole dish, arrange half the lamb slices and half the kidneys on top. Place another potato layer on top; then cover with remaining lamb slices and kidneys. Finish with a layer of potatoes.

2 Combine cornflour mixture, stock, garlic, parsley, wine, rosemary and black pepper and pour over potato slices.

3 Cover and bake for 2¹/₂-3 hours. Uncover and pour over melted butter, return to oven and bake for a further 20 minutes.

Serves 4

Lamb Hot Pot, Braised Pork Shank

Braised Pork Shank

45g (1¹/₂oz) butter

1 pork shank or hock, cut into 8 thick slices by the butcher and tied securely with kitchen string to keep meat attached to bone

2 tblspn olive oil

2 cloves garlic, crushed

2 onions, chopped

4 sticks celery, chopped

185g (6oz) carrots, chopped

2 tspn finely grated lemon rind

2 tspn dried thyme

1 x 250g (8oz) can cannellini beans, drained

300ml (10fl oz) dry white wine

440ml (14fl oz) chicken stock

4 tblspn tomato purée

1 Melt butter in a large, nonstick frying pan over moderate heat. Add pork, brown well on all sides, transfer to a plate. Pour excess butter from frying pan and discard. Heat oil in the pan, add garlic, onions, celery and carrots and sauté for 5 minutes, stirring constantly.

2 Return pork to frying pan, add lemon rind, thyme, beans, wine, stock and tomato purée. Bring to the boil, then simmer, covered, for 2 hours, turning pork occasionally. To serve, remove string from pork, arrange slices on a serving plate, pour sauce over top and serve.

Serves 4

Vietnamese Spring Rolls

Vietnamese Spring Rolls

1 tblspn oil

375g (12oz) minced pork

1 tblspn grated fresh root ginger

1 spring onion, finely chopped

2 tblspn soy sauce

$1/2$ tspn chilli paste

2 tspn honey

185g (6oz) cooked, peeled prawns, finely chopped

90g (3oz) beansprouts

1 tblspn chopped fresh basil

24 wonton wrappers

oil for deep frying

1 Heat oil in a medium frying pan over moderate heat, add pork, ginger, spring onion and soy sauce and cook, for 3 minutes, stirring constantly. Stir in chilli paste, honey, prawns, beansprouts and basil, mix well. Remove from heat and cool to room temperature.

2 Spread 1 tablespoon of pork mixture across the corner of each wonton wrapper. Roll up, tucking in ends, brush edges with a little water to seal.

3 Deep fry wontons for 2 minutes or until golden brown. Drain on paper towels and serve.

Serves 4

Curried Lamb Triangles with Minted Yogurt

45g (1$1/2$oz) butter

1 onion, finely chopped

1 clove garlic, crushed

1 tblspn curry powder

2 tblspn sweet fruit chutney

500g (1lb) minced lamb

3 tblspn tomato purée

125ml (4fl oz) coconut cream, or 45g (1$1/2$oz) creamed coconut mixed with 125ml (4fl oz) warm water

$1/4$ tspn chilli paste

1 packet filo pastry, thawed if frozen

155ml (5fl oz) low fat natural yogurt

30g (1oz) mint leaves

1 Preheat oven to 180°C (350°F, Gas 4). Melt butter in a large frying pan over moderate heat, add onion, garlic and curry powder and cook, stirring occasionally, for 3 minutes. Stir in chutney and lamb and cook until browned. Stir in tomato purée, coconut cream and chilli paste and simmer for 10 minutes.

2 Blend or process mixture to finely chopped ingredients, but not purée.

3 Cut each sheet of pastry into 4 strips, about 10cm (4in) wide. Place a tablespoon of mixture 5cm (2in) up from the bottom of each pastry strip. Flatten filling slightly and fold pastry over filling squarely. Continue to fold pastry upwards in a triangular fashion, all the way to the top. Place triangles on a baking sheet. Melt remaining butter and brush over each triangle. Bake for 15-20 minutes or until golden.

Bacon and Pinenut Crêpes, Curried Lamb Triangles with Minted Yogurt

4 Blend or process yogurt with mint leaves until finely chopped. Serve yogurt with triangles.

Makes about 24

Bacon and Pinenut Crêpes

125g (4oz) plain flour, plus 2 tblspn
1 egg, lightly beaten
500ml (16fl oz) milk
2 tblspn chopped fresh parsley
30g (1oz) butter
60g (2oz) ricotta or cream cheese
90g (3oz) Cheddar cheese, grated
¼ tspn grated nutmeg
4 rindless bacon rashers, chopped
30g (1oz) pinenuts

1 Preheat oven to 180°C (350°F, Gas 4). Sift 125g (4oz) of the flour into a medium bowl, make a well in the centre, then gradually stir in egg and about half the milk to make a smooth batter. Blend or process to remove any lumps if necessary. Stir in parsley.

2 Heat a lightly greased crêpe pan over a high heat. Pour 3 tablespoons of batter into pan and tilt pan to spread batter evenly. Cook until lightly golden on each side. Repeat with remaining mixture to make 8 crêpes.

3 Make filling: Heat remaining milk in a small saucepan. Melt butter in a second saucepan over gentle heat. Stir in remaining 2 tablespoons of flour and cook for 30 seconds, gradually stir in the hot milk, blending well. Stir in ricotta or cream cheese and slowly bring to the boil. Remove from the heat, stir in Cheddar and nutmeg.

4 Cook bacon in a small frying pan in its own fat, add pinenuts, cook until golden. Stir into cheese sauce. Spoon equal amounts of the filling over the crêpes and roll up. Place crêpes in a baking dish and bake for 20 minutes until heated through.

Serves 4

CHICKEN CHOICE

Chicken is a cheap and versatile meat that can be used in many different styles of cooking. Try it in delicious recipes such as Chicken and Rice with Coriander, Chicken Cobbler, or Dijon Dill Chicken.

Bacon Wrapped Chicken Liver Kebabs

185ml (6fl oz) brandy

2 cloves garlic, crushed

500g (1lb) chicken livers

220g (7oz) thin rashers rindless bacon

watercress to serve

1 Place the brandy and garlic in a shallow bowl, add the chicken livers in one layer; marinate for 1 hour.

2 Wrap each chicken liver in a slice of bacon and thread onto skewers.

3 Grill kebabs under moderate heat for about 2 minutes on each side or until cooked through. Serve on a bed of watercress.

Serves 4

Oriental Chicken

4 chicken breasts, skinned and halved

250ml (8fl oz) dry red wine

60ml (2fl oz) olive oil

60ml (2fl oz) soy sauce

30g (1oz) brown sugar

2 tspn ground ginger

1 Place chicken in one layer in a ceramic ovenproof baking dish. Mix wine, oil, soy sauce, sugar and ginger in a bowl and pour over chicken. Cover and refrigerate for at least 2 hours or overnight.

2 Preheat oven to 180°C (350°F, Gas 4). Bake chicken with

marinade in oven for about 40 minutes. Baste from time to time. Remove chicken to a platter and keep warm.

3 Strain marinade into a saucepan and reduce over moderately high heat to about 250ml (8fl oz).

4 Pour some of the reduced marinade over chicken, serve remainder separately in a sauceboat. Serve hot.

Serves 4

Chicken Tacos

8 taco shells

1 tblspn oil

1/2 onion, finely chopped

4 tomatoes, chopped

3 tblspn tomato purée

1 tblspn chopped fresh parsley

375g (12oz) cooked chicken, chopped

125g (4oz) Cheddar cheese, grated

1 Preheat oven to 160°C (325°F, Gas 3). Heat tacos on a large baking sheet in oven for 12 minutes, or warm under a low grill for 2-3 minutes.

2 Meanwhile fry onion in oil in a medium saucepan until soft. Add tomatoes, tomato purée, parsley and onion and cook over moderate heat for 10 minutes. Stir in chicken.

3 Fill each taco with the chicken and tomato mixture, then top with grated cheese. Serve immediately.

Serves 4

Chicken Tacos, Bacon Wrapped Chicken Liver Kebabs

Golden Baked Chicken Wings

1.5kg (3lb) chicken wings

155g (5oz) cornmeal

60g (2oz) grated Parmesan cheese

1/2 tspn paprika

2 tblspn finely chopped fresh coriander

salt

freshly ground black pepper

2 large eggs

2 tblspn cold water

2 tblspn lemon juice

30g (1oz) butter, melted

Marinade

75ml (2^1/2fl oz) freshly squeezed lime juice

75ml (2^1/2fl oz) vegetable oil

1^1/2 tspn Tabasco sauce

^{3}/4 tspn cayenne pepper

1/2 tspn ground coriander

^{3}/4 tspn ground cumin

2 cloves garlic, finely chopped

1/2 onion, finely chopped

1 To make marinade, whisk together lime juice, oil, Tabasco, cayenne, coriander, cumin, garlic and onion. Pour into shallow dish.

2 Remove chicken wingtips and place chicken in marinade, cover and place in refrigerator overnight.

3 Preheat oven to 200°C (400°F, Gas 6). In a bowl, mix together cornmeal, Parmesan, paprika and coriander, season with salt and pepper.

4 In another bowl, beat together eggs, water and lemon juice.

5 Drain chicken wings, discarding marinade. Dip into egg mixture and then coat well with cornmeal mixture. Arrange on baking sheets. Stand for 30 minutes. Drizzle with butter and bake for 35 minutes or until crisp and golden.

Serves 6

Chicken and Rice with Coriander

2 tblspn lemon juice

1 tblspn soy sauce

1 tspn grated fresh root ginger

a few drops Tabasco sauce

1 cooked chicken, skin removed

1 tblspn olive oil

1 small onion, thinly sliced

1 clove garlic, finely chopped

155g (5oz) button mushrooms, sliced

salt

freshly ground black pepper

155g (5oz) long grain white rice

250ml (8fl oz) chicken stock

125ml (4fl oz) dry white wine

60ml (2fl oz) water

3 tblspn chopped fresh coriander

1 Preheat oven to 190°C (375°F, Gas 5). Combine lemon juice, soy sauce, ginger and Tabasco in a large shallow bowl.

2 Cut chicken into 8 serving pieces, add to the bowl, turn pieces to coat thoroughly. Set aside.

3 Heat oil in a large saucepan, add onion and garlic and sauté for about 5 minutes until onion is golden. Add mushrooms and sauté for a further 5 minutes. Season with salt and pepper.

4 Add rice to pan, increase heat and sauté for about 3 minutes until rice becomes translucent. Add stock, wine and water. Stir well and bring to the boil. Transfer to an ovenproof dish, cover and bake in oven for 10 minutes.

5 Using a slotted spoon, place chicken pieces on top of rice, pour over marinade, sprinkle with coriander. Cover and bake for about 10 minutes until chicken is heated through and rice is tender. Serve hot.

Serves 4

Chicken Pineapple Kebabs

250g (8oz) pumpkin or carrots, peeled and cut into 2cm (3/4in) cubes

4 chicken breast fillets, skinned and cut into 2cm (3/4in) cubes

1 x 220g (7oz) can pineapple chunks, drained

2 cloves garlic, crushed

2 tblspn soy sauce

60ml (2fl oz) lemon juice

1 tblspn honey

1 Bring a saucepan of water to the boil, add the pumpkin or carrots and blanch for 3 minutes; drain.

2 Thread chicken cubes onto 8 wooden skewers, adding one pineapple cube and one pumpkin or carrot cube to each.

3 Combine garlic, soy sauce, lemon juice and honey in bowl; brush over kebabs. Grill under moderate heat for 3 minutes each side or until cooked through.

Serves 4

Sweet Chicken Drumsticks with Polenta Crust

8 chicken drumsticks

3 tblspn apricot jam, warmed

185g (6oz) flour

1 tspn salt

90g (3oz) fine polenta (cornmeal)

2 eggs, beaten

oil for deep-frying

1 Brush each drumstick with the jam, then roll in 125g (4oz) of flour. Combine remaining flour with salt and polenta. Coat drumsticks with the beaten eggs, then coat with polenta mixture.

2 Deep fry drumsticks in hot oil for 20 minutes until golden and cooked. Drain on paper towels.

Serves 4

Chicken Pineapple Kebabs, Sweet Chicken Drumsticks with Polenta Crust

Chicken Cobbler

surface. Using a scone cutter, cut out 7 scones and place on top of chicken.

5 Bake until chicken is cooked and scones are risen and golden.

Serves 4

Chicken with Sweetcorn and Cumin

1 tblspn olive oil
2 onions, chopped
4 small chicken pieces
250ml (8fl oz) dry white wine
250ml (8fl oz) chicken stock
250ml (8fl oz) double cream
250g (8oz) sweetcorn kernels
1 tblspn ground cumin

1 Preheat oven to 180°C (350°F, Gas 4). Heat the olive oil in a large frying pan over moderate heat. Add the onions and cook for 2 minutes.

2 Add the chicken and sauté for about 8 minutes until golden brown. Drain the chicken on paper towels and transfer to an ovenproof dish.

3 Pour off the fat from the frying pan and add the wine. Bring to the boil over moderately high heat, scraping up the brown bits from the bottom of the pan. Boil for about 4 minutes until the wine is reduced by half.

4 Stir in the chicken stock, cream, sweetcorn and cumin and cook for a further 5 minutes. Pour the mixture into the ovenproof dish with the chicken and bake in oven for 35 minutes until chicken is cooked.

Serves 4

Variation

This sweetcorn and cumin sauce is also delicious served with herby pork or beef sausages. Sauté the sausages for 2-3 minutes in step 2, and reduce final cooking time to 15-20 minutes.

Chicken with Sweetcorn and Cumin

Chicken Cobbler

60g (2oz) butter
4 chicken breast fillets, cut into 2cm (3/4in) cubes
2 medium potatoes, peeled and cut into 1cm (1/2in) cubes
1 large onion, chopped
2 large carrots, cut into 1cm (1/2in) cubes
3 tblspn flour
250ml (8fl oz) dry white wine
750ml (11/4pt) hot chicken stock
250ml (8fl oz) double cream
2 tblspn tomato purée

Scone Topping

250g (8oz) self-raising flour
2 tblspn dried mixed herbs
30g (1oz) grated Parmesan cheese
30g (1oz) butter, chopped
250ml (8fl oz) milk

1 Preheat oven to 180°C (350°F, Gas 4). Melt butter in a large frying pan over a moderate heat. Add chicken and cook for 3 minutes, stirring constantly.

2 Add potatoes, onion and carrots to pan and cook for 7 minutes, stirring constantly.

3 Stir in the flour, cook for 2 minutes, then add wine, stock, cream and tomato purée. Cook for 10 minutes. Transfer mixture to a large ovenproof dish.

4 To make scone topping, sift flour into a medium bowl. Stir in herbs and cheese, rub in butter with fingertips. Make a well in the centre, add milk and, using a round-bladed knife, stir mixture to a soft, sticky dough. Turn dough onto a lightly floured surface, knead lightly until smooth. Gently press out dough to a 2cm (3/4in) thickness on a lightly floured

Creamy Basil Chicken

625g (1¹/₄lb) boneless chicken breasts, skinned

15g (1/2oz) basil leaves

1 clove garlic

2 tblspn olive oil

salt

2 tblspn white wine vinegar

125ml (4fl oz) double cream

1 Place chicken breasts between layers of heavy-duty plastic food wrap and pound to a 2.5mm (¹/₈in) thickness.

2 Blend basil in a blender or food processor. With machine running, add garlic and blend. Add oil, season with salt and process.

3 Brush one side of chicken with basil-flavoured oil. Place in a preheated dry frying pan, brush top with oil. Cook underside for 1 minute, turn, cook other side. This is best done in batches. Set aside and keep warm.

4 Add vinegar to pan. Cook over a moderately high heat, scraping up any browned bits. Add cream and any juices from chicken and cook for 3 minutes, until mixture coats the back of a spoon, stirring constantly. Season. Spoon sauce over chicken and serve.

Serves 4

Dijon Dill Chicken

1.5kg (3lb) chicken pieces

4 tblspn chopped fresh dill

freshly ground black pepper

90g (3oz) butter, melted

4 tblspn Dijon mustard

1 Preheat oven to 180°C (350°F, Gas 4). Rinse chicken pieces. Dry with paper towels. Rub dill into chicken pieces. Season with pepper.

2 Combine butter and mustard. Arrange chicken pieces skin-side down in a baking dish. Spread tops with half of the butter mixture.

4 Bake in oven for 25 minutes. Turn chicken pieces, spread skin side with remaining mustard butter. Bake for a further 30 minutes or until chicken is cooked and golden. Serve hot.

Serves 4

Curried Chicken Wings with Mushrooms

60g (2oz) butter

8 chicken wings, each separated into two pieces

500g (1lb) button mushrooms, sliced

250ml (8fl oz) double cream

2 tspn mild curry powder

1 tblspn chopped fresh coriander

1 In a medium frying pan, melt butter over moderate heat until sizzling. Add chicken and cook for 15 minutes or until cooked through, stirring frequently. Remove chicken and keep warm.

2 Stir mushrooms and curry powder into frying pan and cook for 3 minutes. Add cream and bring mixture to the boil, then simmer for 10 minutes or until sauce thickens slightly.

3 Add coriander and chicken pieces, mix well.

Serves 4

Hazelnut Chicken

60g (2oz) whole hazelnuts, toasted

4 boneless chicken breasts, skinned

salt

freshly ground black pepper

45g (1¹/₂oz) butter

125ml (4fl oz) dry white wine

250ml (8fl oz) double cream

1 tspn lemon juice

Curried Chicken Wings with Mushrooms, Chicken Drumsticks with Mango Sauce

1 Rub off skins off nuts and chop. Place chicken breasts between layers of heavy-duty plastic food wrap and pound until about 1cm (1/2in) thick. Season.

2 Melt butter in a large frying pan, add chicken breasts and sauté for 8 minutes or until golden, turning once. Remove and keep warm.

3 Add wine to pan, cook over a high heat, scraping up any browned bits. Reduce liquid to 2 tablespoons. Add cream and cook until it has thickened slightly, stirring constantly. Add lemon juice and season.

4 Pour sauce over chicken and sprinkle with toasted hazelnuts.

Serves 4

Chicken Drumsticks with Mango Sauce

60g (2oz) butter
8 chicken drumsticks
1 x 425g (13 1/2oz) can mango slices
60ml (2fl oz) double cream
1/4 tspn grated nutmeg

1 Preheat oven to 180°C (350°F, Gas 4). Melt butter in a large frying pan, add chicken drumsticks and cook for 2 minutes, stirring frequently.

2 Remove chicken from pan, place in a baking dish and bake for 15-20 minutes or until cooked.

3 Drain mango slices, reserving mango juice. Add juice to frying pan. Stir over moderate heat until juice boils and thickens slightly. Remove from heat, strain and return sauce to frying pan.

4 Add cream and nutmeg and slowly bring to the boil, then simmer for 8 minutes. Add the mango slices to sauce. Serve chicken with sauce.

Serves 4

Roasted Chicken with Rosemary and Carrots

2 Cut chicken into 1cm (^{1}/2in) wide strips. Add to the bowl and toss gently to coat well. Cover and refrigerate until ready to serve. Serve chilled.
Serves 4

Chicken Salad with Mango and Onion Dressing

500g (1lb) chicken breasts

1 mango, peeled, stoned and flesh coarsely chopped

2 tblspn lemon juice

1 tblspn red wine vinegar

1 tblspn olive oil

salt

freshly ground black pepper

lettuce leaves

^{1}/2 small Spanish onion, chopped

1 Place chicken breasts under a preheated grill and cook for about 8 minutes until chicken is cooked, turning once. Set aside to cool.

2 Combine mango flesh, lemon juice, vinegar and oil in a blender or food processor. Purée until smooth and season with salt and pepper.

3 Arrange lettuce leaves on a platter.

4 When chicken is cool, remove the skin and cut flesh into strips. Arrange on lettuce leaves.

5 Stir onion into mango mixture and pour over chicken. Cover salad and refrigerate for 30 minutes before serving.
Serves 6

Roasted Chicken with Rosemary and Carrots

1.5kg (3lb) oven-ready chicken, giblets removed

5 rosemary sprigs

5 carrots, cut in half lengthwise

3 tblspn redcurrant jelly

30g (1oz) butter

1 tspn white pepper

1 Preheat oven to 180°C (350°F, Gas 4). Wash chicken and place 3 of the sprigs of rosemary into cavity. Place chicken in a large roasting tin with carrots alongside.

2 Melt redcurrant jelly with butter and pepper in a small saucepan over moderate heat. Chop the remaining rosemary sprigs into small pieces and add to melted jelly mixture.

3 Brush mixture over chicken. Cook chicken and carrots in oven for 1-1^1/2 hours until chicken is cooked, basting regularly with jelly mixture, and turning carrots frequently.
Serves 4

Chicken and Apple Coleslaw

^{1}/2 small white cabbage, shredded

1 Granny Smith apple, unpeeled and cut into 1cm (^{1}/2in) cubes

125ml (4fl oz) salad dressing

375g (12oz) cooked boneless chicken breasts, skinned

1 Combine cabbage, apple and salad dressing in a salad bowl.

Red Cabbage and Chicken Salad with Spanish Onion Dressing

750g (1¹/₂lb) boneless chicken breasts, skinned

1 tblspn chopped fresh thyme

salt

freshly ground black pepper

1 small Spanish onion

¹/₂ small red cabbage, leaves separated

75ml (2¹/₂fl oz) olive oil

60ml (2fl oz) red wine vinegar

1 Cut chicken into 2.5cm (1in) cubes. Sprinkle with thyme and season with salt and pepper.

2 Slice onion very thinly, separate rings. Rinse red cabbage, drain, dry, refrigerate.

3 Heat half of the oil in a frying pan. Add chicken and sauté for about 5 minutes until cooked through. Remove from pan. Keep warm. Add vinegar to pan, scraping up any browned bits.

4 Remove from heat, stir in onion and remaining oil. Season with salt and pepper.

5 Arrange red cabbage on a serving platter, top with warm chicken and spoon over Spanish onion mixture.

Serves 4

Variations

Radiccio or Cos lettuce may be used instead of red cabbage. The salad may be extended further by adding other vegetables of your choice such as cooked green beans, sweetcorn, or quartered tomatoes. Alternatively, add crisp crumbled bacon when serving.

Crunchy Chicken Salad

4 cooked chicken breast fillets, cut into strips

250ml (8fl oz) soured cream

125ml (4fl oz) mayonnaise

4 sticks celery, cut into 4cm (1¹/₂in) long thin strips

¹/₂ bunch spring onions, chopped

60g (2oz) pecan nuts or walnuts, roughly chopped

parsley sprig for garnish

1 Place chicken strips in a large bowl.

2 Whisk soured cream and mayonnaise together until smooth and add to chicken.

3 Add celery, spring onions and pecan nuts or walnuts and toss well. Refrigerate before serving. Serve garnished with parsley.

Serves 4

Crunchy Chicken Salad

LIGHT MEALS

If you have had a substantial meal at lunchtime, you might like to try one of these tasty light meals as a change from beans on toast, or scrambled eggs. Most of the recipes are based on vegetables, eggs and cheese and include dishes such as Soufflé Tomatoes, or Herb Omelette with Pitta Bread.

Scotch Eggs

4 hard-boiled eggs

500g (1lb) sausagemeat, divided into 4 rounds

1 egg, lightly beaten

pinch cayenne pepper

125g (4oz) dried breadcrumbs

oil for deep-frying

parsley sprig for garnish

1 Carefully shell the eggs. Pat out each round of sausagemeat, with damp hands. Place each egg on a sausagemeat round and shape it carefully around the egg so that the egg is completely enclosed.

2 Roll in the combined beaten egg and cayenne pepper, then in the breadcrumbs.

3 Heat the oil in a saucepan over moderate heat and deep fry each egg for about 3 minutes until golden brown and cooked through. Drain on paper towels. Serve garnished with parsley.

Serves 4

Egg Mousse

1/2 x 11g (1/3oz) sachet powdered gelatine

2 tblspn cold water

1/2 x 440g (14oz) can beef consommé

3 hard-boiled eggs

2 tblspn soured cream

2 tblspn double cream

60ml (2fl oz) mayonnaise

1/2 tspn curry powder

1/2 tspn mango chutney

salt

freshly ground black pepper

125g (4oz) cherry tomatoes, halved

fresh snipped chives

1 Sprinkle gelatine onto cold water in a small bowl. When spongy, melt over hot water. Stir mixture into consommé, mix well.

2 Chop eggs. Whisk soured cream and double cream together until soft peaks form. Stir in mayonnaise, curry powder and mango chutney juice. Add eggs and three quarters of the consommé and gelatine mixture. Mix well, add salt and pepper to taste and divide between 4 ramekins. Allow to almost set.

3 Arrange cherry tomatoes and chives on top of ramekins. Spoon over remaining consommé mixture and chill in a refrigerator for at least 1 hour before serving.

Serves 4

Scotch Eggs

Tasty Cheese Triangles, Mini Olive Quiches

Mini Olive Quiches

2 sheets ready-rolled frozen puff pastry, thawed
125ml (4fl oz) milk
3 eggs, lightly beaten
60ml (2fl oz) double cream
30g (1oz) Cheddar cheese, grated
1 tspn paprika
10 green stuffed olives, sliced

1 Preheat oven to 190°C (375°F, Gas 5). Line four 15cm (6in) individual loose-bottomed flan tins with the pastry. Prick bases with a fork and line with greaseproof paper. Fill with dried beans or baking beans and bake blind in oven for about 5 minutes. Lower oven temperature to 180°C (350°F, Gas 4).

2 Meanwhile combine the milk, eggs, cream, cheese and paprika, mix well. Divide the olives between the pastry cases and pour over the egg mixture.

3 Bake in oven for 15-20 minutes or until risen and golden.
Serves 4

Tasty Cheese Triangles

560ml (18fl oz) milk
100g (3^1/2oz) semolina
125g (4oz) Cheddar cheese, grated
2 tblspn finely chopped fresh parsley
1 tblspn finely snipped fresh chives
1 egg, lightly beaten
125g (4oz) dried breadcrumbs
30g (1oz) grated Parmesan cheese
oil for frying

1 Slowly bring the milk to the boil over moderate heat in a large saucepan. While stirring, very slowly add the semolina. Simmer mixture for 5 minutes, stirring constantly.

Dutch Open Ham Sandwich with Fried Egg

30g (1oz) butter
4 slices fresh bread
mustard to taste
4 thin slices ham
4 eggs, fried
8 cocktail onions, drained
2 gherkins, drained and thinly sliced
2 tomatoes, sliced
parsley sprigs for garnish

1 Butter bread and spread with a thin coating of mustard.

2 Place a slice of ham on each piece of bread, top with an egg and arrange onions, slices of gherkin and tomato on top. Garnish with parsley and serve immediately.
Serves 2

White Cheese Dip, Soufflé Tomatoes

2 Melt the butter in a medium saucepan over moderate heat, stir in the flour and cook for 1 minute. Gradually stir in the cream and season with salt and pepper. Cook for about 2 minutes until thick and smooth, stirring constantly. Remove pan from heat. Mix in the cheese and egg yolks.

3 Beat egg whites in a bowl until stiff peaks form, fold a little into the cheese mixture to lighten, then fold in remainder. Spoon the mixture into the tomatoes, filling each to about three-quarters full.

4 Place tomatoes in a buttered baking dish and cook for about 15-20 minutes or until soufflés have risen.

Serves 4

White Cheese Dip

60g (2oz) butter

200g (6¹/₂oz) cream cheese

155g (5oz) feta cheese

freshly ground black pepper

¹/₄ tspn grated nutmeg

1 tblspn lemon juice

1 tblspn finely snipped fresh chives

crusty bread for serving

1 Melt the butter in a large saucepan over a moderate heat. Add the cream cheese, feta cheese, black pepper and nutmeg. Cook for 5 minutes or until cheeses soften, stirring constantly.

2 Stir in lemon juice. Spoon cheese dip onto a flat plate, sprinkle with chives and serve at once with chunks of crusty bread.

Serves 4

Variations
This cheesy soufflé mixture also tastes delicious piled into lightly blanched pepper or aubergine shells, or hollowed-out baked potatoes.
Alternatively, spread it on toast and grill until golden. If preferred, replace the Cheddar cheese with other cheese of your choice.

2 Remove from heat and stir in the Cheddar cheese, parsley and chives. Spread mixture evenly over a Swiss roll tin to the depth of 1cm (¹/₂in) and refrigerate for about 20 minutes until set and very cold.

3 Slice the mixture into triangles. Dip each one in the beaten egg, then coat with the combined breadcrumbs and Parmesan.

4 Heat the oil in a frying pan. Add the triangles and cook for about 30 seconds each side until light golden. Drain on paper towels, and serve.

Serves 4

Soufflé Tomatoes

8 tomatoes

30g (1oz) butter

2 tblspn flour

185ml (6fl oz) double cream

salt

freshly ground black pepper

125g (4oz) mature Cheddar cheese, grated

3 eggs, separated

1 Preheat oven to 180°C (350°F, Gas 4). Slice the tops off the tomatoes and scoop out pulp. Discard tomato tops and pulp. Invert tomatoes on paper towels and set aside to drain.

Chicken and Courgette Pancakes

125g (4oz) plain flour

1 egg

375ml (12fl oz) milk

185g (6oz) courgettes, grated

2 tblspn chopped fresh parsley

30g (1oz) butter

250ml (8fl oz) double cream

1/4 tspn grated nutmeg

60ml (2fl oz) white wine

250g (8oz) cooked chicken, cut into small pieces

1 tblspn snipped fresh chives

parsley sprigs and strips of red pepper for garnish

1 Place flour, egg and milk in a blender or food processor and blend until smooth. Tip into a bowl, stir in the courgettes and parsley and set aside for 15 minutes.

2 To make pancakes, melt butter in frying pan over moderate heat. Pour about 4 tablespoons of the courgette mixture into the frying pan and cook until golden on both sides. Repeat with the remaining mixture. Keep pancakes hot.

3 Heat the cream in a medium saucepan over moderate heat. Add the nutmeg and wine and simmer mixture until sauce has thickened slightly. Stir in the chicken and chives, heat through and serve mixture over pancakes. Garnish with parsley and red pepper.

Serves 4

Potato, Bean and Bacon Fry

250g (8oz) piece of smoked bacon, rind removed, cut into 1cm (1/2in) cubes

8 boiled potatoes, cut into 2cm (3/4in) cubes

375g (12oz) cooked chickpeas or red kidney beans

pickle to serve

1 Place bacon cubes in a large, heavy-based frying pan and sauté over a moderately low heat until fat runs freely and cubes are crisp and golden. Remove bacon from pan with a slotted spoon and reserve.

2 Add potatoes to the frying pan, turn the heat up to moderately high and sauté until golden on all sides, turning occasionally. Add beans to frying pan, mix in well and sauté for a further 3 minutes.

3 Mix in reserved bacon and heat through for a further 2 minutes. Serve hot with pickle.

Serves 4

Macaroni and Beef Gratin

315g (10oz) macaroni

375g (12oz) cottage cheese

250ml (8fl oz) soured cream

250g (8oz) cooked roast beef, finely chopped

1/2 onion, chopped

2 sticks celery, chopped

3 tblspn chopped fresh parsley

1 tspn Worcestershire sauce

30g (1oz) fresh breadcrumbs

60g (2oz) mature Cheddar cheese, grated

1 Preheat oven to 180°C (350°F, Gas 4). Cook macaroni in a saucepan of salted boiling water until nearly tender or *al dente*, drain.

2 Combine macaroni with cottage cheese, soured cream, beef, onion, celery, parsley and Worcestershire sauce, toss to blend.

3 Spoon into a buttered 1.5 litre (2 1/2pt) ovenproof dish. Combine breadcrumbs with Cheddar and sprinkle over macaroni.

4 Bake in oven for 30 minutes or until top is crisp and golden. Allow to stand at room temperature for 5 minutes before serving.

Serves 4

Chicken and Courgette Pancakes

Creamy Cheese Roulade

Herb Omelette with Pitta Bread

1 egg
1 tspn cold water
salt
freshly ground black pepper
30g (1oz) butter
1 tblspn mixed finely chopped fresh chives, parsley and dill
1 pitta bread
1 lettuce leaf, shredded
1 tomato, sliced
1/2 fennel bulb, finely sliced
1/4 small cucumber, finely sliced
watercress sprigs

1 Lightly beat egg, water, salt and freshly ground pepper to taste. Heat an omelette pan, melt 15g (1/2oz) butter, then add egg mixture.

2 Using a spatula, draw mixture from the sides of the pan to the centre to allow uncooked egg to run underneath. Leave for a few seconds, sprinkle mixed herbs over the top, loosen sides and fold into three. Slip omelette onto a plate to cool.

3 Split pitta bread almost through lengthwise, spread open on a flat surface. Butter both sides with remaining butter. Arrange lettuce on one side, slide omelette on top. Cover with slices of tomato, fennel and cucumber and add watercress sprigs. Sandwich pitta bread together again and serve.

Serves 1

Kitchen Tip
If pimientos are not available, place 2 large red peppers under a hot grill for 10-12 minutes until the skins have blackened and charred. Place peppers in a paper bag for 10 minutes, then peel away skins and cut peppers into strips.

Creamy Cheese Roulade

5 eggs, separated
2 tspn Dijon mustard
125g (4oz) Cheddar cheese, grated
45g (1 1/2oz) fresh breadcrumbs
Filling
250g (8oz) cream cheese, softened
250g (8oz) pimiento, sliced, or see Kitchen Tip
dill sprigs for garnish

1 Preheat oven to 180°C (350°F, Gas 4). Line a Swiss roll tin with greased greaseproof paper.

2 Beat egg yolks with mustard until light and whisk leaves a trail when lifted. Fold in Cheddar. Beat the egg whites until stiff, then fold into the yolk mixture with the breadcrumbs. Spread into the prepared tin and bake in oven for 15 minutes until risen and golden.

3 Run a knife around the edge of the tin and turn roulade out onto a sheet of greaseproof paper. Remove paper used to line tin. Cool, then roll up the roulade from one of the short sides, using the paper as a guide. When cool, cover and refrigerate.

4 Unroll roulade. Spread a layer of cream cheese over surface. Scatter pimientos over the top, re-roll and slide onto a serving platter. Keep in a cool place until ready to serve. Serve sliced, garnished with dill.

Serves 4

Herb and Cheddar Cheese Soufflé

Herb and Cheddar Cheese Soufflé

50g (1³/₄oz) butter

3 tblspn flour

300ml (10fl oz) milk

230g (7¹/₂oz) Cheddar cheese, grated

¹/₄ tspn grated nutmeg

4 tblspn chopped fresh herbs

salt

freshly ground black pepper

4 eggs, separated

1 Preheat oven to 180°C (350°F, Gas 4). Melt the butter in a large saucepan over a moderate heat. Stir in the flour and cook for 1 minute. Gradually add the milk and stir constantly over a gentle heat until sauce is thick and smooth.

2 Stir in the Cheddar cheese, nutmeg, herbs and salt and pepper. Mix well, then beat in the egg yolks one at a time.

3 Beat the egg whites in a bowl until soft peaks form, fold 2 tablespoons into the cheese mixture, then fold in remainder.

4 Pour mixture into a buttered 1 litre (1³/₄pt) soufflé dish and bake in oven for 25-30 minutes until risen and golden.

Serves 4

Kitchen Tip
To ensure even rising when cooking soufflés always use a straight-sided buttered soufflé dish and fill no more than three-quarters full. Use a clean dry finger to clear away mixture from the sides of the dish and make a gutter. Serve a soufflé as soon as it is taken from the oven or it will collapse.

Sausage and Pasta Frittata

185g (6oz) sausagemeat

1 red pepper, cut into strips

2 tblspn olive oil

1 small onion, thinly sliced

1 clove garlic, crushed

315g (10oz) cooked pasta shells

6 eggs

60g (2oz) grated Parmesan cheese

2 tblspn chopped fresh parsley

salt

freshly ground black pepper

1 Place sausagemeat in a large heavy-based frying pan and cook over moderate heat until lightly browned, stirring with a wooden spoon to break up any lumps. Pour off any fat. Add red pepper and continue cooking for about 10 minutes until softened. Transfer mixture to a large bowl.

2 Heat half the oil in the pan, add onion and garlic, sauté for about 5 minutes until tender. Add cooked pasta and stir over heat for 1 minute until heated through. Add mixture to sausagemeat and red pepper in bowl. Wipe frying pan clean with paper towels.

3 In another bowl, beat eggs, cheese and parsley until well combined. Season with salt and pepper. Pour over sausage and pasta mixture, mix well.

4 Heat remaining oil in the frying pan, add sausage, pasta and egg mixture, cook over a moderately low heat for about 10 minutes until top begins to set and edges start to brown. Place a large plate or flat saucepan lid over the pan, invert frittata and slide back into the pan to cook for a further 5 minutes to brown underside. Cut into wedges to serve.

Serves 6

Mediterranean Frittata

125ml (4fl oz) olive oil

2 medium potatoes, thinly sliced

1 large onion, thinly sliced

1 clove garlic, crushed

2 small aubergines, thinly sliced

salt

2 medium courgettes, thinly sliced

2 red peppers, chopped

8 eggs, beaten

freshly ground black pepper

2 tblspn chopped fresh marjoram or 1 tspn dried marjoram

1 Preheat oven to 180°C (350°F, Gas 4). Heat the oil in a roasting tin in oven for 5 minutes. Add potatoes, onion and crushed garlic and bake for 20 minutes.

2 While potato is cooking, sprinkle aubergine slices with salt, leave to drain in a colander for 10 minutes. Rinse and pat dry with paper towels.

3 Place aubergine and courgette slices on top of potato and bake in oven for 5 minutes.

4 Sprinkle red peppers over the top. Pour beaten eggs over vegetables, season with salt, pepper and marjoram. Bake for a further 20 minutes or until a knife inserted into the centre comes out clean and the top is golden brown. Cut in squares or slices to serve.

Serves 8

Aubergine Omelette

1 small aubergine

salt

oil for frying

1/2 clove garlic

6 eggs

freshly ground black pepper

15g (1/2oz) butter

1 Cut aubergine into 4cm (1½in) strips. Sprinkle strips with salt, leave to drain in a colander for 10 minutes. Rinse and pat dry with paper towels.

2 Heat 1cm (½in) oil in a frying pan, add garlic and half of the aubergine strips. Cook gently for about 3 minutes until golden, stirring occasionally. Remove aubergines with a slotted spoon, leave garlic in pan. Drain aubergines on paper towels and keep warm while frying the remaining strips. Discard garlic.

3 Beat eggs with salt and pepper in a bowl. Melt butter in a large omelette pan, add egg mixture and tilt pan to allow uncooked egg to run underneath.

4 When almost cooked, sprinkle with aubergine strips. Fold omelette, slide onto a heated platter. Serve hot.
Serves 2

Vegetable Frittata

30g (1oz) unsalted butter

1 tblspn vegetable oil

1 onion, finely chopped

1 clove garlic, thinly sliced

250g (8oz) mushrooms, thinly sliced

185g (6oz) peas

250g (8oz) broccoli, broken into small florets

6 slices ham, 2.5mm (1/8in) thick, cut into bite-sized pieces

8 eggs, lightly beaten

30g (1oz) grated Parmesan cheese

salt

freshly ground black pepper

1 Melt butter with oil in a large frying pan which can be used under the grill. Sauté onion and garlic for 5 minutes Add mushrooms and cook for 1 minute. Add peas, broccoli and ham, sauté for a further 1 minute.

2 Combine eggs, Parmesan, salt and pepper in a bowl. Mix well. Pour over vegetables in pan, then reduce heat and cook frittata for about 7 minutes until eggs have almost set.

3 Place frittata under preheated grill for 2-3 minutes until golden brown. Cut into wedges and serve.
Serves 6-8

Broccoli and Bacon Frittata

8-10 small broccoli florets

125g (4oz) piece of smoked bacon

2 medium onions, thinly sliced

8 eggs, beaten

salt

freshly ground black pepper

1 Steam, boil or microwave broccoli until just tender but still crisp, set aside.

2 Cut bacon into small cubes and cook in a large frying pan until fat runs freely and bacon is crisp. Remove bacon with a slotted spoon, drain on paper towels.

3 Cook onions in bacon fat remaining in pan for about 8 minutes until transparent. Add broccoli and bacon, toss lightly, then pour over beaten eggs. Season with salt and pepper, cook over a gentle heat until eggs have almost set.

4 Place frittata under a grill for 1-2 minutes or until top is golden brown. Cut into wedges and serve at once.

Serves 6-8

Cheese and Herb Bread Pudding

125g (4oz) butter, softened

8 slices medium sliced bread, crusts removed

3 eggs

600ml (1pt) milk

60g (2oz) Cheddar cheese, grated

125ml (4fl oz) single cream

1 tblspn chopped fresh herbs

1/2 tspn paprika

1 Preheat oven to 180°C (350°F, Gas 4). Butter the bread generously, cut each slice of bread into 4 triangles and decoratively arrange the bread into a buttered 1 litre (1¾pt) ovenproof dish.

2 Combine eggs, milk, cheese, cream and herbs, pour mixture over the bread and sprinkle with paprika. Allow to stand for 30 minutes.

3 Bake pudding in oven for 45 minutes until set and golden.
Serves 4

Cream Cheese Crêpes

125g (4oz) plain flour

3 eggs, lightly beaten

250ml (8fl oz) milk

375g (10oz) cream cheese

3 tblspn snipped fresh chives

1/2 tspn grated nutmeg

125g (4oz) sweetcorn kernels

2 tblspn finely chopped fresh parsley

1 Sift flour into a medium bowl, gradually stir in eggs and milk and stir until smooth. Strain batter to remove lumps if necessary.

2 Heat a medium frying pan over moderate heat, grease lightly and pour in about 60ml (2fl oz) batter to make a crêpe. Cook each side until a light golden colour. Repeat with remaining mixture. Keep crêpes hot.

3 To make filling, place cream cheese, chives and nutmeg in a blender or food processor and blend until smooth. Stir in the sweetcorn and parsley.

4 Place about 3 tablespoons of mixture onto each crêpe, roll up and serve at once.
Serves 4

Kitchen Tip
To cut down on last-minute preparation time, make up a batch of crêpes in advance. Layer between sheets of greaseproof paper, wrap in foil or a polythene bag and freeze for up to 3 months. To use, simply reheat from frozen. Alternatively, keep a packet of ready-made crêpes in the store cupboard for quick and easy meals.

Cheese and Herb Bread Pudding,
Cream Cheese Crêpes

Index

Editorial Coordination: Merehurst limited
Cookery Editors: Polly Boyd, Jenni Fleetwood, Katie Swallow
Editorial Assistant: Sheridan Packer
Production Manager: Sheridan Carter
Layout and Finished Art: Stephen Joesph
Cover Photography: David Gill
Cover Design: Maggie Aldred

Published by J.B. Fairfax Press Pty Limited
80-82 McLachlan Avenue
Rushcutters Bay 2011
A.C.N. 003 738 430
Formatted by J.B. Fairfax Press Pty Limited
Printed by Toppan Printing Co, Singapore

JBFP 249 A/UK
Includes Index
ISBN 1 86343 118 7
ISBN 86343 116 0 (Set)

DISTRIBUTION AND SALES ENQUIRIES
Australia: J.B. Fairfax Press Pty Limited
Ph: (02) 361 6366 Fax: (02) 360 6262
United Kingdom: J.B. Fairfax Press Limited
Ph (0933) 402330   Fax (02) 402234